EARLY DAYS

OF THE

PRESBYTERIAN BRANCH

OF THE

Holy Catholic Church,

IN THE STATE OF MINNESOTA,

BY

EDWARD D. NEILL,

DELIVERED, IN SUBSTANCE, BEFORE THE
SYNOD OF MINNESOTA, IN

First Presbyterian Church, Minneapolis,

SEPTEMBER 26, 1873.

MINNEAPOLIS:
JOHNSON & SMITH, STEAM PRINTERS.
1873.

EARLY DAYS

OF THE

PRESBYTERIAN BRANCH

OF THE

Holy Catholic Church,

IN THE STATE OF MINNESOTA,

BY

EDWARD D. NEILL,

DELIVERED, IN SUBSTANCE, BEFORE THE
SYNOD OF MINNESOTA, IN

First Presbyterian Church, Minneapolis,

SEPTEMBER 26, 1873.

MINNEAPOLIS:
JOHNSON & SMITH, STEAM PRINTERS.
1873.

HISTORICAL DISCOURSE.

"Appoint John Knox Bishop of Rochester; he will prove a whetstone to the Archbishop of Canterbury," was the message to Cecil from the Duke of Northumberland. If the appointment had been made, there might have been no room for the work which the Presbyterian Church has performed during the last three centuries.

Upon many points Knox and Archbishop Cranmer were in harmony. In accordance with the suggestion of Calvin, the English Church published a summary of Christian doctrine, and had expressed the teachings of the Apostle Paul in the seventeenth of the "Thirty-Nine Articles," which was fully accepted by the Scotch Reformer.

Nor did they differ in relation to the orders of the ministry. The latter, notwithstanding his position, explicitly declared, that there were but two orders, and that the ordination of the Swiss and French Churches was as valid as that of the Church of England, for it was not until the reigns of the vacillating Stuarts, that the Church of England assumed the intolerable position, that the ordination of a priest of Rome was valid, while that of a Presbyterian minister was invalid.

But notwithstanding this general agreement, Knox could not feel that his mission was in that Church. He believed that it was the design of the English Court to fetter the Church and not to permit it to have "free course" in the work of restoration to primitive purity. He did not oppose, but approved of a liturgy, yet he was pained by the retaining of Saints' days in Edward the Sixth's Book of Prayer, and also by the forcing upon the conscience things, that could not be clearly deduced from the precept and practice of Christ and the Apostles. He moreover thought that the source of civil power was in the people, and they had the right to depose wicked and treacherous rulers. While admitting that the Church of England had broken away from the stall of popery, he declared that the halter was still around her neck, and he sought Scotland, his native land, as a more acceptable field of labor than the See of Rochester. By the earnest, thorough work there performed, room was made in the world, for that branch of the Catholic Church, which is in part represented by the Synod of Minnesota.

From the first, the Presbyterian has been a missionary church. The first General Assembly of 1560 was composed of only twelve ministers, five of whom were without a local charge, and moved through the land, preaching the gospel to the poor, planting churches, and appointing lay readers.

Since that time its strength has been in earnest preaching of Christ, and in carrying the truth to those who will not send for preachers. It is eminently fitting that we should take a retrospect of Presbyterianism in the Valley of the Upper Mississippi, from the Falls of St. Anthony, now in the centre of the City of Minneapolis, for in this vicinity was the gospel first preached to the wild Dakotah, as well as to the civilized white man of Minnesota, by members of the Presbyterian branch of the Church.

During the days of the French dominion in the Mississippi Valley, sincere and earnest Franciscans and Jesuits of the Church of Rome visited this region, and endeavored to convert the savages to Christianity. Their advent, heralded by the sympathizing Canadian voyageurs, at first made a deep impression. But the children of the wilderness soon grew weary of the pictures and bells, and swinging censers of the "black gowns." Shea, in his interesting and highly colored history of the Roman Catholic missions among the Indians, remarks that "Father Menard had projected a Sioux mission; Marquette, Allonez, Dreuilletes, all entertained hopes of realizing it, and had some intercourse with that nation, but none of them ever succeeded in establishing a mission."

About a century after Father Guignas left the French fort "Beauharnois," nearly opposite Maiden's Rock, on the shores of Lake Pepin, another effort was made under a simpler and more primitive form of Christianity, to evangelize the tribes in the region of the great lakes and the Upper Mississippi River.

In the month of June, 1820, the Rev. Dr. Morse, father of the distinguished inventor of the telegraph, visited and preached at Mackinaw, and in consequence of statements published by him, upon his return, a Presbyterian Missionary Society in the State of New York sent a graduate of Union College, the Rev. W. M. Ferry, father of the present United States Senator from Michigan, to explore the field. In 1823 he had established a large boarding school composed of children of various tribes, and here some were educated who became wives of men of intelligence and influence at the capital of Minnesota. After a few years, it was determined by the Mission Board to modify its plans, and in the place of a great central station, to send missionaries among the several tribes to teach and to preach.

In pursuance of this policy, the Rev. Alvan Coe, and J. D. Stevens, then a licentiate, made a tour of exploration, and arrived on September 1, 1829, at Fort Snelling. In the journal of Major Lawrence Taliaferro, which is in possession of the Minnesota Historical Society, I find the following entry: "The Rev. Mr. Coe and Stevens reported to be on their way to this post, members of the Presbyterian Church looking out for suitable places to make missionary establishments for the Sioux and Chippeways, found schools, and instruct in the arts and agriculture."

The Agent, although not at that time a communicant of the Church, welcomed these visitors, and afforded them every facility in visiting the Indians. On Sunday, the 6th of September, the Rev. Mr. Coe preached twice in the Fort, and the next night held a prayer-meeting at the quarters of the commanding officer. On the next Sunday he preached again, and on the 14th, with Mr. Stevens and a hired guide, returned to Mackinaw by way of the St. Croix river. During this visit the Agent offered for a Presbyterian mission the mill which then stood on the site of Minneapolis, and had been erected by the soldiers, as well as a farm at Lake Calhoun, which had been established for the benefit of the Dakotahs.

On the 8th of September he addressed the following letter to the Rev. Joshua T. Russell, Secretary of the Board of Missions of Presbyterian Church, Philadelphia, Pa.:

"REV. SIR: It having been represented to me by the Rev. Alvan Coe, that it is very desirable on the part of the Board of Missions of the Presbyterian Church, to form an establishment at this post, and also within the heart of the Chippeway country bordering on the Upper Mississippi, for the purposes of agriculture, schools, and the development of the light and truths of the Christian religion to the unhappy aborigines of this vast wilderness.

"As my views fully accord in every material point with those of Messrs. Coe and Stevens, I can, in truth, assure the Board through you, sir, of my determination heartily to co-operate with them in any and every measure that may be calculated to insure success in the highly interesting and important objects to which the attention of the Society has been so happily directed.

"I have recommended to the Government to appoint a special sub-agent to reside at Gull Lake, to superintend the general concerns of the most warlike and respectable portion of the Chippeways of the Mississippi and its tributary waters above Lake Pepin, thereby to lessen their visits to this Agency, it being desirable to prevent their coming in contact too often with their old enemies, the Sioux.

"Should the Society form a missionary establishment on the waters of the St. Croix, some of which communicate with Rum River of the Mississippi, and a special agent or sub-agent, the influence of whom might be necessary to the more efficient operations of the missionary families there located, I have no doubt but that the Government would be willing to appoint one for the special duty, if requested by the Society, accompanied by explanatory views on the subject.

"As to an establishment for the Sioux of this Agency, it would be in the power of the Society to commence operations, without much expense, at the Falls of St. Anthony, where there is a good grist and saw-mill, with suitable buildings, at present going into decay for the want of occupants. I would cheerfully turn over my present infant colony of agriculturists, together with their implements and horses, etc., to such an establishment."

It was not, however, till the year 1834, that any formal attempt was made to instruct them in the morality of the Bible. The Rev. Samuel W. Pond, who had been a layman and school teacher in Galena, Illinois, hearing accounts of the Dakotahs from Red River emigrants, became interested in their welfare, and wrote to his brother, Gideon H. Pond, then a young man in their native place in Connecticut, proposing that they should cast their lot with the Dakótahs, and try to do them good.

The proposition was accepted, and in the spring of 1834, constrained only by the love of Christ, provided with neither brass, nor scrip, nor purse, he joined his brother at Galena, and embarking on board of a steamer, arrived at Fort Snelling in

May. They stated their plans to Mr. Taliaferro, the Dakotah Agent, and were treated with kindness by him and Major Bliss, the commander of the Fort. Without aid or eneouragement from any missionary society, they proceeded to the east shore of Lake Calhoun, on the banks of which and Lake Harriet dwelt small bands of Dakotahs, and with their own hands erected a rude cabin on the site of a building in more recent times occupied by Charles Musou.

About this period, a native of South Carolina, a graduate of Jefferson College, Pennsylvania, the Rev. T. S. Williamson, M.D., who previous to his ordination had been a respectable physician in Ohio, was appointed by the American Board of Commissioners of Foreign Missions to visit the Dakotahs, with the view of ascertaining what could be done to introduce Christian instruction. Having made inquiries at Prairie du Chien and Fort Snelling, he reported the field was favorable.

The Presbyterian and Congregational Churches, through their joint Missionary Society, appointed the following persons to labor in Minnesota: Rev. Thomas S. Williamson, M.D., missionary and physician; Rev. J. D. Stevens, missionary; Alexander Huggins, farmer; and their wives; Miss Sarah Page, and Lucy Stevens, teachers; who were prevented during the year 1834, by the state of navigation, from entering upon their work.

During the winter of 1834–35, a pious officer of the army exercised a good influence on his fellow officers and soldiers under their command. In the absence of a chaplain or ordained minister, he, like General Havelock of the British army in India, was accustomed not only to drill the soldiers, but to meet them in his own quarters, and reason with them "of righteousness, temperance and judgment to come."

In the month of May, 1835, Dr. Williamson and mission band arrived at Fort Snelling, and were hospitably received by the officers of the garrison, the Indian Agent, and Mr. Sibley, then a young man, who had recently become Agent of the Fur Company, at Mendota.

On the 27th of the month Dr. Williamson was called upon to unite in marriage Lt. Edmund A. Ogden, a young officer, to Eliza Edna, daughter of Capt. Gustavus A. Loomis, the first ceremony of the kind performed by a clergyman north of Prairie du Chien.

It was not until May, 1838, that Rev. E. G. Gear, of the Episcopal branch of the Church, became post Chaplain.

On the 11th of June, in the quarters at the Fort occupied by Dr. Williamson, a meeting was held to organize a church. Upon inquiry it was found that there were twenty-two persons ready to unite in an organization, and six of these, one of whom was the young Lieutenant Ogden, had never been communicants.

Four elders were elected, among whom were Capt. Gustavus Loomis and Samuel W. Pond. The next day, a lecture preparatory to administering the communion, was delivered, and on Sunday the 14th, the first organized church in the Valley of the Upper Mississippi assembled for the first time in one of the Company rooms of the Fort. The services in the morning were conducted by Dr. Williamson. After prayer, singing and reading of the Holy Scriptures, those proposing to become communicants for the first time, came forward as their names were called, and made profession of their faith. A sermon was then preached by Dr. Williamson, and after prayer by Mr. Stevens, the four elders were ordained. The afternoon service commenced at 2 o'clock. The sermon of Mr. Stevens was was upon a most appropriate text, 1st Peter, ii. 25; "For ye were as sheep going astray, but are now returned unto the Shepherd and Bishop of your souls."

After the discourse the sacrament of the Lord's Supper was administered.

At a meeting of the Session on the 31st of July, Rev. J. D. Stevens, missionary, was invited to preach to the church "so long as the duties of his mission will permit, and also to preside at all the meetings of the Session." Captain Gustavus Loomis was elected Stated Clerk of the Session, and they resolved to observe the monthly concert of prayer on the first Monday of each month, for the conversion of the world.

Two points were selected by the missionaries as proper spheres of labor. Mr. Stevens and family proceeded to Lake Harriet, and Dr. Williamson and family, in June, 1835, proceeded to Lac-qui-Parle.

Dr. Williamson came down from Lac-qui-Parle on a visit to the Fort, on the 11th of June, 1836, and after preaching on the next Sunday, gave notice that on the following Sunday he would administer the communion. The preparatory lecture was delivered on Friday, the 17th, before the church convened at the Mission House, on Lake Harriet, and on the 19th the Lord's Supper was observed. At a meeting of the Session, on the 28th of October, it was resolved that Divine Service should hereafter be held at the Mission House, Lake Harriet, every Sunday morning, and in the Fort, at 6 o'clock, Sunday evening.

On the 30th of December there was an examination of the Mission School at Lake Harriet. The examiners were Major Taliaferro and Henry H. Sibley, and among the spectators were Major Loomis, Lt. Ogden, and their families, and Surgeon Emerson, whose servant was then, the since historic slave Dred Scott, whose wife had been owned by Agent Taliaferro.

On the 15th of September, 1836, a Presbyterian Church was organized at Lac-qui-Parle, a branch of that in and near Fort Snelling, and Joseph Renville, a mixed blood of great influence, became a communicant. He had been trained in Canada by a Roman Catholic priest, but claimed the right of private judgment. Before he became acquainted with the missionaries, he sent for a Bible in the French language, and requested those connected with him in the fur trade also to procure a clerk for him who would be able to read it. This Bible, among the first ones brought to Minnesota, was valuable for its antiquity. It was printed at Geneva, in 1588, and had a Latin preface by John Calvin. In 1853 I requested the missionaries to procure this valuable book for the Minnesota Historical Society. One of the sons of Mr. Renville brought it to the mission house at Lac-qui-Parle, but before it could be forwarded the mission house and contents were all destroyed by fire. Mr. Renville's wife was the first pure Dakotah of whom we have any record that ever joined the Church of Christ. In 1841 Renville was elected Elder. This church has never become extinct, although its members have been necessarily nomadic. After the treaty of Traverse des Sioux, it was removed to Hazlewood. Driven from thence by the outbreak of 1862, it has became the parent of other churches, over one of which John Renville, a descendant of the elder at Lac-qui-Parle, is the pastor.

About the time that Renville was ordained an elder in the church, Father Ravoux, recently from France, a sincere and earnest priest of the Church of Rome, visited Lac-qui-Parle. He came to Mendota in the autumn of 1841, and after a brief sojourn with Father Galtier, who had erected St. Paul's Chapel, which has given the name of St. Paul to the capital of Minnesota, he ascended the Minnesota River, and visited Lac-qui-Parle.

Bishop Loras, of Dubuque, wrote the next year of his visit as follows: "Our young missionary, Mr. Ravoux, passed the winter on the banks of Lac-qui-Parle, without any other support than Providence, without any other means of conversion than a burning zeal, he has wrought in the space of six months a happy revolution among the Sioux. From the time of his arrival he has been occupied night and day in the study of their language. * * * * When he instructs the savages, he speaks to them with so much fire whilst showing them a large copper crucifix which he carries on his breast, that he makes the strongest impression upon them."

The impression, however, was evanescent, and he soon retired from the field, and no more efforts were made in this direction by the Church of Rome. The young Mr. Ravoux is now the highly respected Vicar of the Roman Catholic Diocese of Minnesota. and justly esteemed for his simplicity and unobtrusiveness.

During the year 1837, Mr. G. H. Pond offered his services as farmer and teacher at Lac-qui-Parle, and Mr. S. W. Pond became a teacher in the mission at Lake Harriet. The mission band was also greatly strengthened this year by the arrival of Rev. Stephen R. Riggs, a graduate of Jefferson College, Pa., and his wife. Mr. Riggs soon proceeded to Lac-qui-Parle, and was there associated with Dr. Williamson.

In the year 1838 a circumstance occurred which ultimately led to the dispersion of the Dakotahs at Lake Harriet, and a removal of the mission. On the 2d of August, Hole-in-the-Day, an Ojibway chief, who had killed thirteen of the Lac-qui-Parle Dakotahs, visited Fort Snelling with a few associates, to the regret of the officer in command, Major Plympton. The next evening Mr. Samuel W. Pond met Agent Taliaferro at Lake Harriet, and told him that a number of Indians from Mud Lake had gone to Baker's trading house, near the Fort, to attack the Ojibways. The Agent hastened to the spot, and arrived just as the first gun was fired by the Dakotahs, killing one of the Ojibways. A Red Lake Ojibway in return shot the murderer just as he was scalping his victim. The commanding officer of the Fort as soon as possible brought the Ojibways within its walls. On the evening of the 6th the Ojibways were ferried across the river and ordered to go home immediately. On the 29th of June, 1839, Hole-in-the-Day again visited the Fort with hundreds of Ojibways, and on the 1st of July they met the Dakotahs at the Falls of St. Anthony, and after smoking the pipe of peace, the majority of the Ojibways proceeded homeward; but some of the Pillager band passing over to Lake Harriet, secreted themselves until after sunrise on July 2d, when they surprised Meekah, a Dakotah on his way to hunt, and scalped him.

Rev. J. D. Stevens hurried to the Fort with the intelligence. Immediately one hundred and fifty Dakotahs were on the war path, panting for vengeance, and hurrying after the Ojibways, who had ascended the Mississippi; and the next day there was a fight at Rum River, and ninety of the latter were killed. Another party also went across the country to St. Croix river, and overtook a band of Ojibways in the ravine where the penitentiary at Stillwater stands, and killed twenty-one and wounded twenty-nine. After this the Dakotahs were afraid to live at Lake Harriet, and soon abandoned the place, and encamped on the Minnesota river near Fort Snelling. The missionaries also removed to Baker's trading post, between the Fort and Minnehaha.

At the commencement of 1841 there was at Lac-qui-Parle, Rev. Thos. S. Williamson and wife, Rev. S. R. Riggs and wife, Alexander G. Huggins, *Farmer*, and wife; Fanny Huggins, *Teacher*. At Fort Snelling was Rev. Samuel W. Pond and wife, and Gideon H. Pond and wife. At both stations the Dakotah language was diligently studied. Rev. S. W. Pond had prepared a dictionary of three thousand words and also a small grammar. The Rev. S. R. Riggs was also engaged in translating the Scriptures. In a letter dated February 24, 1841, he writes, "Last summer, after returning from Fort Snelling, I spent five weeks in copying again the Sioux vocabulary which we have collected and arranged at this station. It contained then about 5500 words, not including the various forms of the verbs. Since that time the words collected by Dr. Williamson and myself, have, I presume, increased the number to six thousand. * * * * * In this connection I may mention that during the winter of 1839-40, Mrs. Riggs, with some assistance, wrote an English and Sioux vocabulary containing about three thousand words. This one of Mr. Renville's sons and three of his daughters are engaged in copying. In committing the grammatical principles of the language to writing, we have done something at this station, but more has been done by Mr. S. W. Pond."

Steadily the number of Indian missionaries increased in Minnesota, and in 1851, when the lands of the Dakotahs west of the Mississippi were ceded to the whites, they were disposed as follows:

Lac-qui-parle, Rev. S. R. Riggs, Rev. M. N. Adams, *Missionaries;* Jonas Pettijohn, Mrs. Fanny Pettijohn, Mrs. Mary Ann Riggs, Mrs. Mary A. M. Adams, Miss Sarah Rankin, *Assistants.*

Traverse des Sioux, Rev. Robert Hopkins, *Missionary;* Mrs. Agnes Hopkins, Alexander G. Huggins, Mrs. Lydia P. Huggins, *Assistants.*

Shakpay, Rev. Samuel W. Pond, *Missionary;* Mrs. Sarah P. Pond, *Assistant.*

Kaposia, Rev. Thos. Williamson, M.D., *Missionary and Physician;* Mrs. Margaret P. Williamson, Miss Jane S. Williamson, *Assistants.*

Red Wing, Rev. John F. Aiton, Rev. Joseph W. Hancock, *Missionaries;* Mrs. Nancy H. Aiton, Mrs. Hancock, *Assistants.*

On July 4th, 1851, while a treaty was in progress with the Indians at Traverse des Sioux, the resident missionary, Rev. Robert Hopkins, was drowned while bathing.

The mission station at Kaposia was established in 1846, in consequence of a brawl occasioned by whisky purchased of some low fellows who lived in rude huts around the log chapel of St. Paul. In a drunken revel the Kaposia chief had been shot in the arm, and alarmed at the deterioration produced by intoxicating liquor, he went to Mr. Bruce, the Indian Agent, at Fort Snelling, and asked that a school might be established in his band. At the request of the Agent, in November Dr. Williamson came down from Lac-qui-Parle, and became a resident at Little Crow's village. Although a missionary among the Dakotahs, he watched with interest the development of the obscure hamlet of Saint Paul, and determined to have a school established there. To obtain a teacher, he wrote the following letter in 1847 to the President of the National Education Society:

"My present residence is on the utmost verge of civilization, in the northwestern part of the United States, within a few miles of the principal village of white men in the territory that we suppose will bear the name of Minnesota, which some would render 'clear water', though strictly it signifies slightly turbid or whitish water.

"The village referred to has grown up in a few years in a romantic situation on a high bluff of the Mississippi, and has been baptized by the Roman Catholics, by the name of St. Paul. They have erected in it a small chapel, and constitute much the larger portion of the inhabitants. The Dakotahs call it Im-ni-ja-ska (white rock), from the color of the sandstone which forms the bluff on which the village stands. This village has five stores, as they call them, at all of which intoxicating drinks constitute a part, of what they sell. I would suppose the village contains a dozen or twenty families living near enough to send to school. Since I came to this neighborhood I have had frequent occasion to visit the village, and have been grieved to see so many children growing up entirely ignorant of God, and unable to read his word, with no one to teach them. Unless your Society can send them a teacher, there seems to be little prospect of their having one for several years. A few days since I went to the place for the purpose of making inquiries in reference to the prospect of a school. I visited seven families, in which there were twenty-three children of proper age to attend school, and was told of five more in which were thirteen more that it is supposed might attend, making thirty-six in twelve families. I suppose more than half of the parents of these children are unable to read themselves, and care but little about having their children taught. Possibly the priest might deter some from attending, who might otherwise be able and willing.

"I suppose a good female teacher can do more to promote the cause of education and true religion than a man. The natural politeness of the French (who constitute more than half the population) would cause them to be kind and courteous to a female, even though the priest should seek to cause opposition. I suppose she might have twelve or fifteen scholars to begin with, and if she should have a good talent of winning the affections of children (and one who has not should not come), after a few months she would have as many as she could attend to.

"One woman told me she had four children she wished to send to school, and that she would give boarding and a room in her house to a good female teacher, for the tuition of her children.

"A teacher for this place should love the Saviour, and for his sake should be willing to forego, not only many of the religious privileges and elegancies of New England towns, but some of the neatness also. She should be entirely free from prejudice on account of color, for among her scholars she might find not only English, French and Swiss, but Sioux and Chippewas, with some claiming kindred with the African stock.

"A teacher coming should bring books with her sufficient to begin a school, as there is no book-store within three hundred miles."

In answer to his wish, Miss Harriet E. Bishop visited the mission house at Kaposia, and was introduced by him to the citizens of St. Paul as their first school teacher.

In October, 1848, a native of the City of Philadelphia, who after his ordination preached among the miners in the lead mines, about fifteen miles from Galena, wrote to Rev. A. Kent, the senior member of the Galena Presbytery: "I have been informed that you intend to go to Minnesota for the purpose of organizing a church in Stillwater, if the way be open. I do not know what your arrangements may be about the supply of that distant field, but if you can fill my present post, I am ready to go as the pioneer in that region. My wife and I are contented enough here, but it is almost too civilized. The latter fact would make it desirable to some, that would not like to go so far from the luxuries and comforts of the East. If, then, you are of the opinion that I and mine are the persons suited for a new field, I am at your disposal."

The Rev. Mr. Kent made the proposed visit, but the time did not seem favorable for a church organization at Stillwater, and it was postponed. Before the opening of navigation, next spring, the Territory of Minnesota had been created by Congress, and St. Paul designated as its capital.

The Presbytery of Galena, at a meeting held about the 1st of April, resolved "that the Rev. E. D. Neill visit Minnesota in company with Rev. A. Kent, and that if the field please him, he be released from his charge at Elizabeth, and be permitted to labor in Minnesota."

In accordance with this resolution, Rev. Mr. Neill came to St. Paul in April. At that time, and until after the treaty of Traverse des Sioux, there were Indian villages and mission stations at Kaposia and Red Wing, below St. Paul, and at Oak Grove and Shakpay, on the Minnesota River, within a half days' ride.

Mr. Neill's first sermon was preached in a little school house erected for the school that had been projected by Dr. Williamson, and which Miss Bishop had taught, and his text was "How is it that thou being a Jew, askest drink of me which am a woman of Samaria?"—John iv. 9.

The Rev. B. F. Hoyt, a local Methodist preacher, was the only religious teacher in the place.

In May Mr. Neill went to Philadelphia, as Commissioner of Galena Presbytery to the General Assembly of the Presbyterian Church, and soon after his return commenced the erection of the first Protestant Church edifice in the white settlements of Minnesota. It was a small frame building situated on Washington Street, and was completed about the last of August. The funds for the building were given by a few of his relatives and personal friends in the city of Philadelphia. The following May it was destroyed by fire.

At the first Thursday evening religious lecture in this chapel with no previous understanding, there were present the Rev. W. T. Boutwell, the first missionary to the Ojibways of the Mississippi, and chaplain of the expedition to the sources of the Mississippi, in 1832, and the Rev. Gideon H. Pond, who with his brother, as we have seen, was the first to attempt to do good to the Dakotahs near Fort Snelling.

A short period before Mr. Neill came to Saint Paul, Lieut. Col. Gustavus Loomis was ordered to Fort Snelling as commanding officer, after an absence of several years. The first Stated Clerk of the Session of the Church organized at Fort Snelling in 1835, his love for the synagogue had not diminished in 1849, and he extended to the young minister of St. Paul a cordial welcome.

In July, 1849, Mr. Neill received the following note from Fort Snelling:

"The Colonel commanding this garrison, and several citizens amongst whom are Major Murphy, Mr. Prescott and others respectfully invite, and hope it will be convenient for you to preach to us occasionally, if it would not interfere with other appointments. We will endeavor to defray all expenses and add our mite towards supporting the Gospel."

It was customary for Mr. Neill to preach at St. Paul in the morning, and at St. Anthony or Fort Snelling in the afternoon of Sunday. During the first six months the only contributions made for the support of the gospel were from Fort Snelling. Col. Loomis gave ten dollars, Philander Prescott ten dollars and John H. Stevens five dollars.

On the 4th of October, Rev. J. C. Whitney, a graduate of Union Theological Seminary, arrived at Stillwater, and took charge of the St. Croix valley.

A meeting of the male professors of religion attending the preaching of Mr. Neill in St. Paul, was held on the evening of November 26th, 1849.

Mr. Neill being present, he was asked to state his denominational preferences. He declined, alleging as a reason that he was commissioned by a Board composed of two sister denominations, simply "to preach the gospel," and that he did not wish to bias them by stating his ecclesiastical connection, as he was ready to labor for their welfare, whatever form of church government they might choose. After prayer it was resolved unanimously, "That we form ourselves into a church, under the name of 'The First Presbyterian Church of St. Paul.'"

The second church organized was at Stillwater. The Rev. J. C. Whitney being at that time a licentiate, invited Rev. W. T. Boutwell, a Congregational minister and formerly missionary of the A. B. C. F. M. among the Ojibways, and Rev. E. D Neill, to assist him in organizing a church. The meeting was held on the afternoon of December 8th, 1849. At the suggestion of Rev. W. T. Boutwell it was unanimously voted that the church be called "The First Presbyterian Church of Stillwater."

The first communion in the First Presbyterian Church at St. Paul was on the first Sunday of January in 1850. Dr.

Williamson of Kaposia mission, was present, and several Indian converts partook of the sacrament.

During the last week in December, the Rev. Dr. Williamson of Kaposia, and Rev. Gideon H. Pond of Oak Grove, revived the old church at Fort Snelling, and Colonel G. Loomis and P. Prescott were chosen Elders, and Rev. G. H. Pond elected Pastor ; and it was decided hereafter that it should be called the " Oak Grove Church."

After the small wooden church edifice in St. Paul was destroyed by fire, Mr. Neill preached in an unplastered ware-room built of rude boards, that stood at the corner of Wapa-shah street, where Cathcart & Co.'s store is, and in this rude building Fredrika Bremer the Swedish authoress, once wor-shipped with the congregation, while on the same Sunday, Dr Williamson was preaching to some Indians in a log house then occupied by the late Joseph R. Brown, which stood opposite on the site of Ingersoll's block of stores.

During the winter of 1849–50, Mr. Neill preached every other Sunday afternoon at the Falls of Saint Anthony, and at that time his congregation there, was larger than at Saint Paul. The building in which the service was held, was the first district school house, and still stands not far from the new Methodist Church on University Avenue.

In July, 1850, Rev. W. T. Wheeler, a member of the Wabash Association of Congregational ministers, and formerly mission-ary of the A. B. C. F. M., on the Gaboon river, in Africa, com-menced preaching there, by Mr. Neill's request. His congre-gation was interested in him, and a prayer-meeting sustained. Without any extraneous influence, he thought it proper to form a church. His preferences were for the Congregational polity, but about three-fourths of the members had letters from or were connected with Presbyterian churches, and with-out a thought about the matter, it was unanimously resolved that the church be called "The First Presbyterian Church of Saint Anthony."

After a brief period the Rev. Charles Seccombe succeeded Mr. Wheeler, and in time succeeded in persuading the congregation to drop the name of Presbyterian, and it is now known as the Congregational Society of Minneapolis, E. D.

The Dakotah missionaries before the formation of white settlements, were united in an independent Dakotah Presbytery, the present Dakotah Presbytery of the Synod.

In pursuance of a resolution of the Synod of Peoria, the "Presbytery of Minnesota" comprising the churches in the white settlements, was organized on November 1st, 1850. As long as the entire region between the Mississippi and Missouri was occupied by the Indians, the extension of Presbyterial limits was not practicable.

In time, Rev. G. H. Pond of Oak Grove, who had concluded to remain at the old mission station and preach to the whites, who were beginning to make claims upon the recently ceded lands in his vicinity, was transferred from the Indian or Dakotah Presbytery to the Presbytery of Minnesota.

In October, 1851, the Rev. J. G. Riheldaffer, the present Moderator of the Synod, and who occupies the pulpit with me to-night, arrived in Saint Paul, and in February, 1852, organized the Second Presbyterian Church in that city, now designated as the "Central."

At the close of the summer of 1853, the roll of Minnesota Presbytery was—

Ministers.	*Churches.*	*Members.*
Edw. D. Neill,	Saint Paul	35
Jos. C. Whitney,	Stillwater	14
John C. Sherwin,	La Crosse	20
Gideon H. Pond,	Oak Grove	13
	Kaposia	4
	Minneapolis	15

Rev. G. H. Pond, in the summer of 1852 delivered the first sermon, at the house of Mr. John H. Stevens, to the white settlers on the west side of the Falls of Saint Anthony, and continued to watch over the people there for many months, besides attending to his duties at Oak Grove. On the 22d of May, 1853, after a sermon by Mr. Pond, the First Presbyterian Church of Minneapolis was organized, the first Christian church in the white settlements of Minnesota west of the Mississippi. On the 2d of July the Presbytery of Minnesota convened in Minneapolis, and received the church under its care. Among the corresponding members were Rev. A. G. Chester, D. D., of Buffalo. Shortly after his return to his home, he wrote as follows: "My dear Neill—We have shipped the bell for Minneapolis, and directed it to you. * * * * * It is a very fine one, weighing 511 pounds, and has all the appurtenances. The donor is the Hon. James Wadsworth of this city. I wish they would give their place his name. I think it would be very appropriate, and a very good name. It might be productive."

During the summer of 1853, the brick church erected in 1850, for the First Presbyterian Church of St. Paul, was enlarged by the addition of forty pews. In February, 1854, Rev. Edward D. Neill was unanimously called to be pastor, but declined for several reasons, among others the fact that he had a few weeks before, written to M. W. Baldwin, of Philadelphia, after whom the Baldwin School,* incorporated in 1853, had been named, proposing to enlarge its sphere of operations, and to devote his life to the building up of a College in the Valley of the Upper Mississippi.

Mr. Neill, however, continued to preach for the church until 1855, when the Rev. J. R. Barnes supplied the pulpit until the spring of 1856. During the summer of that year, the Rev. John Mattocks was called to the pastorate. In 1854, the Rev. James Thomson of Indiana, began to preach at Mahkahto, and united with the Presbytery of Minnesota.

*The Baldwin School at first largely consisted of girls. The whole number of pupils enrolled, until January, 1854, was 71, and of these only 28 were boys. After a brief period it seemed expedient to organize a separate department

Rev. Henry M. Nichols also united with the Presbytery, and became pastor at Stillwater, in the place of Rev. J. C. Whitney, who had been installed over the church at Minneapolis.

In the spring of 1855, at a meeting of the friends of the projected College for Minnesota, held in the city of Philadelphia, M. W. Baldwin being in the chair, and among others present, the Rev. Albert Barnes, and Rev. Thomas Brainerd, D. D., the Rev. Edward D. Neill was elected President. During the summer an edifice for the Grammar School of the College was commenced at Saint Paul, opposite the residence of W. L. Banning.

The duties of Mr. Neill as President elect of the College not interfering with his preaching, and the district in which the academic building was situated being remote from any church edifice, the following circular was issued :

"The Presbyterian Mission that was commenced in April, 1849, and discontinued in consequence of the formation of the

for the boys, as a nucleus for a College. In a letter from the founder to Mr. Baldwin, he says: "Already, you will perceive by looking at the Catalogue, that there are quite a number of boys attached to the girls' school. Now there must be a College in this portion of the Mississippi Valley. The picturesqueness of the scenery will make it a classic spot for students. "For the sum of $5,000 a building can be erected which would serve for the purpose of preparatory grammar school, a chapel on Sunday, and a lecture room during winter nights, to which young men may be attracted from the saloons and gambling establishments. I propose that there shall be a young man to act as tutor to the grammar school, and one College professor, who shall hear recitations, lecture during winter evenings, and preach in the chapel. * * * I propose the institution, comprising the classical and scientific departments of the Baldwin School, shall be called Calvary College. I also propose to resign my position as minister of the First Church, and hold the position of Professor of English Literature and History in the Baldwin or Calvary College."

The plan was approved by Mr. Baldwin, and also by the founder's old pastor, the Rev. Albert Barnes. In deference to the Puritan prejudice against the naming of institutions after localities associated with the life of Jesus, the male department of the Baldwin School was incorporated as the "College of Saint Paul," instead of Calvary. The development of the College was impeded by the financial revulsion of 1857, and then again by the breaking out of the rebellion in 1861.

In 1864, by an Act of the Legislature, the two institutions were consolidated, with a provision that the Preparatory Classical Department should be known as the "Baldwin School." This school was re-opened at St. Anthony's Falls in 1872, and preliminary steps have been taken to make it the preparatory department of Macalester College, of which Mr. Neill is the President.

First Presbyterian Church on November 26th, of the same year, will be resumed by the Rev. Edward D. Neill. As the only part of the city entirely destitute of church privileges, is that beyond Eagle street, service will be held every Sunday afternoon at fifteen minutes after 3 o'clock, in the lower room of the district school house on Walnut street, commencing November 25, 1855."

The congregation from the first was unexpectedly large, and during the last week in December a church was organized. On the 23d of December, Mr. Neill preached upon the Centurion who built a synagogue, and at the close made the following allusion to Joseph Wakefield, who left a legacy of $500 for church extension, which was used in purchasing a building site for the new enterprise.

"Eighteen months ago I visited the office of a young man then residing here, and was pained to see on his table the pretended revelations of the Poughkeepsie seer, Davis, in which false philosophy he expressed some interest.

"A few days after, he came and sat with me under the grove of oaks now within the enclosure of my present residence. Looking down at the buildings which were beginning to dot the plateau of upper St. Paul, he remarked that it would soon be filled with a busy population. In reply I said that I hoped at no distant day to see a church spire adorn the loveliest plain of the city."

"In a few months his health began to fail, and he returned to his native State, Rhode Island. Gradually he approached the grave. At first he sought relief from weariness and despondency by the perusal of exciting fictitious literature, but at length, by the persuasion of a Christian brother, he commenced to read the New Testament, and soon saw its beauty and simplicity and sublimity, and unreservedly put his trust in Jesus, and exercised the faith of the Centurion.

"As he approached the dark valley he expressed the wish that $500 might be placed in my hands for church extension. The time has come to use it, and it is appropriate that about the first anniversary of his death we should organize another church."

The little band that assembled to organize the church, agreed that it should be called the "House of Hope," the name given by the Dutch Captain De Vries to the locality now known as Hartford.

The first English church there, was formed by the eminent Hooker who resigned his first charge in Massachusetts, and went to Connecticut, to use his own language, "In view of the increasing emigration, for whose sake he deemed it wise to make more extensive room."

To make more extensive room for the increasing population of St. Paul was the motive that led to the formation of this church, and its first membership, with one exception, was composed of those who had never been connected with any church in that city.

In May, 1857, the Presbytery of Minnesota numbered ten ministers, distributed as follows:

Ministers.	*Churches.*	*Members.*
Edward D. Neill,	House of Hope	17
Joseph C. Whitney	Minneapolis	55
Gideon H. Pond,	Oak Grove	22
Henry M. Nichols,	Stillwater, 1st	22
Charles S. LeDuc	Hastings	20
John Mattocks,	St. Paul, 1st	53
Daniel Ames,	Winona	39
J. W. Hancock,	Red Wing	30
W. A. McCorkle,	Superior	5

In the spring of 1857, the Westminster Church, of Minneapolis, was organized in connection with what was then the other branch of the Presbyterian Church. The next year the Presbytery of Blue Earth was formed, to which the Rev. James Thomson* of Mahkahto, was transferred.

*Rev. James Thompson died at Mankato the day after this discourse was delivered.

At a meeting of the General Assembly of the Presbyterian Church held in Chicago in May, 1858, the following action was taken relative to the erection of the Synod of Minnesota:

"*Resolved*, 1. That the Presbyteries of Blue Earth and Minnesota be directed to meet at Saint Paul, Minnesota, in the First Presbyterian Church on the second Wednesday of September, 1858, at 7 o'clock P. M., with the view of uniting, if the way be prepared, with the Presbytery of Dakota, in the organization of a Synod.

"*Resolved*, 2. That the Stated Clerk of the Assembly address a letter to the Presbytery of Dakota, inviting them to meet with the Presbyteries of Blue Earth and Minnesota, at the above time, and if the way be prepared, to be incorporated with them in a Synod under the care of the General Assembly.

"*Resolved*, 3. That in the event of compliance with this invitation by the Presbytery of Dakota, the Presbyteries of Blue Earth, Minnesota and Dakota, shall then and there become a Synod under the name of the Synod of Minnesota, and that the Rev. Thomas Williamson, or in case of his absence the oldest minister present, shall preach a sermon, and preside until a new Moderator be chosen."

In accordance with these resolutions the three Presbyteries met at the time and place specified, and there organized the Synod of Minnesota, to which name the body addressed by me to-night, has succeeded.

At the formation of the Synod the following ministers were present:

Presbytery of Dakota—Thomas S. Williamson, Samuel W. Pond, and Moses Adams. *Absent*, Stephen R. Riggs, John F. Aiton.

Presbytery of Minnesota—Edward D. Neill, Joseph C. Whitney, Gideon H. Pond, Henry M. Nichols, Charles S. Le Duc, John Mattocks, and J. W. Hancock. *Absent*, Marcus Hicks and Francis A. Griswold.

Presbytery of Blue Earth—Samuel G. Lowry, James Thomson, and Jacob E. Conrad. *Absent*, Gardiner K. Clark, Daniel Ames, Edward D. Holt, and Theophilus Lowry.

More remains to be said of the Early Days of Presbyterianism in Minnesota, which will be unfolded by my colleague, in his historical discourse, appointed to be delivered at the next session of the Synod.

How grateful ought we to be, that so many of those who laid the foundations of our branch of the Church in Minnesota, are still alive. As the roll of the Synod was called at the opening of this session, Pond, Williamson, Riggs, Adams, Hancock, of the old Dakotah Mission, answered to their names. While for years they sowed in tears, they now reap in joy, Their own children, notwithstanding they were born amid savages, have been educated, and three have succeeded their fathers as preachers of glad tidings to the Dakotahs.

The growth of our branch of Zion is encouraging. In the year 1858, after more than twenty years hard labor, but eighty persons of Dakotah blood had united with the Church of Christ, but since the troubles of 1862, about eight hundred of that tribe profess the religion of Jesus, and are connected with the Indian churches of Dakotah Presbytery.

In 1858 there were not more than three or four hundred white persons enrolled, now there are over four thousand communicants in connection with the Synod.

Let us not be cast down. Our mission is to please God, not to please men. We are to study the Word, and declare the whole counsel of God, and in time the fruit will surely appear.

www.ingramcontent.com/pod-product-compliance
Lightning Source LLC
LaVergne TN
LVHW011138110826
845150LV00008B/2394

* 9 7 8 1 4 1 8 1 9 3 8 2 9 *